let
YOUR
light
SHiNE
MATTHEW 5:16

11813607R00063

Made in the USA
Monee, IL
17 September 2019